westermann

Workbook 3

Herausgegeben von
Gisela Ehlers

Erarbeitet von
Gisela Ehlers, Anna Van Montagu,
Matthias Muth, Michaela Schönau,
Hannelore Tait

Auf der Grundlage der Ausgaben
Bumblebee 3/4 (2013/2014) und
Bumblebee 1-4 (2014-2016)
von Gisela Ehlers, Grit Kahstein, Christina Meindl,
Ursula Michailow-Drews, Anna Van Montagu,
Matthias Muth, Michaela Schönau, Hannelore Tait,
Anne Zeich-Pelsis

Muttersprachliche Beratung
Vanessa Magson-Mann

Illustriert von
Juliane Assies, Oda Ruthe, Friederike Schumann
sowie Matthias Berghahn, Andrea Dölling,
Jutta Garbert, Angela Glökler, Heike Heimrich,
Gabie Hilgert, Elisabeth Holzhausen, Karoline Kehr,
Ulf Marckwort, Isabelle Metzen

Contents

TB	Textbook	**Fö**	Förder-Kopiervorlage
WB	Workbook		
CD	Teacher's Audio-CD	**Fo**	Forder-Kopiervorlage
FC/WC	Flashcards/Wordcards		
SC	Storycards	**KV**	Kopiervorlage
L	Lehrkraft		
SuS	Schülerinnen und Schüler		

Rote Wörter stehen fest: Merke sie dir.
Schwarze Wörter kannst du austauschen.
So entsteht ein neuer Satz.

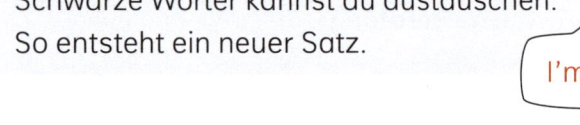 I'm 8.

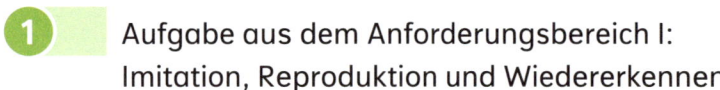 I'm 9.

1 Aufgabe aus dem Anforderungsbereich I:
Imitation, Reproduktion und Wiedererkennen

1 Aufgabe aus dem Anforderungsbereich II:
Reproduktion, erste Konstruktionsversuche
und Erkennen von Zusammenhängen

1 Aufgabe aus dem Anforderungsbereich III:
Zunehmend eigenständige Konstruktion

👂 listen

👆 point

👄 talk/tell/speak/sing/practise/ask

📖 read/look up/look at/find

✏️ write/fill in/label/number/circle/tick

🖌️ draw/colour/create/mark/complete

✒️ match

👓👓 Work/Compare with a partner.

👓 Do a role play./Act it out.

🎲 Play the game.

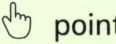 language tip

Welcome

1 👂 👆 Listen and point.

1		2		3		4	
5		6		7		8	
9		10		11		12	
13		14		15		16	

2 👤 ✏️ 👀 Read and number. Compare with a partner.

	jeans		hamburger		computer
	cornflakes		mountain bike		T-shirt
	basketball		popcorn		toaster
	pool		skateboard		hot dog

> Nomen werden im Englischen klein geschrieben.

3 ✏️ Do you know more English words?

shorts

Colours and numbers

1 👂 Listen to the song.

2 🖌 👄 Colour the circles. Sing the song.

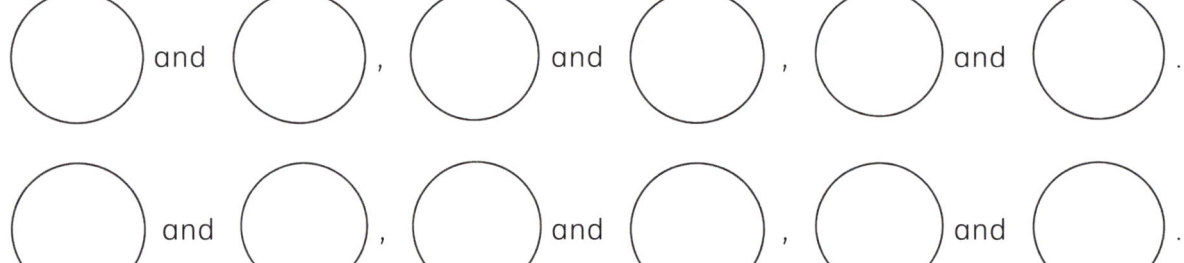

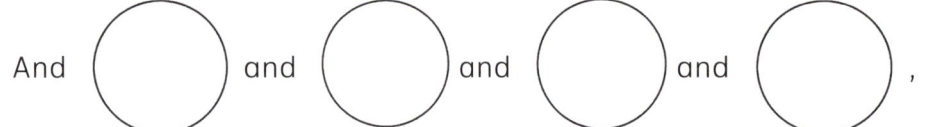

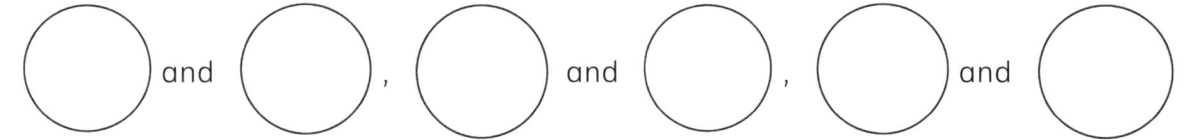

3 👂 🖌 Listen and colour.

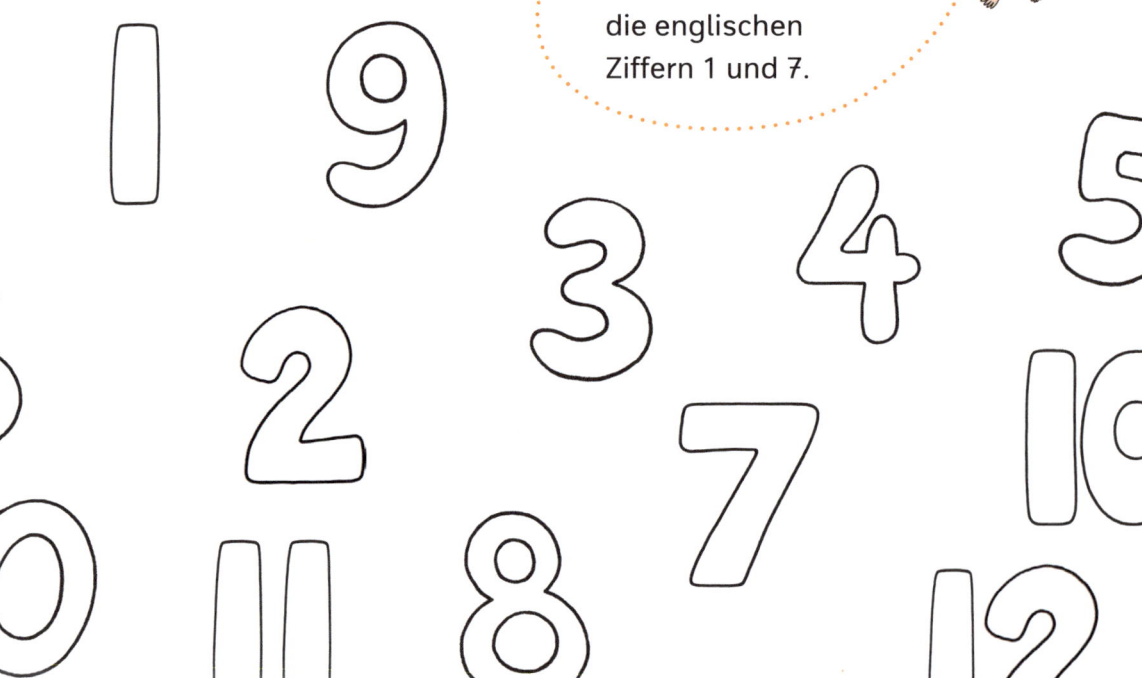

So schreibt man
die englischen
Ziffern 1 und 7.

CD 4-6
Fö/Fo 2-3

LET'S PRACTISE!   **About me**

1 ✏ Fill in the words.

2 📖 Read the dialogue.

3 👀 👂 👄 Practise the dialogue.

My name's =
My name is

What's your
_____ ?

you

I'm fine.

How are
_____ ?

name

My favourite
colour **is** green.

How _____
are you?

My name's Miriam.

What's your favourite
_____ ?

colour

It's 913576.

number

What's your phone
_____ ?

old

I'm seven.

At school

These are scissors.

1 🖉 Label the school things.

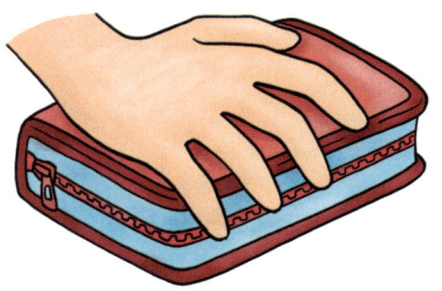

It is a _____ .

These are _____ .

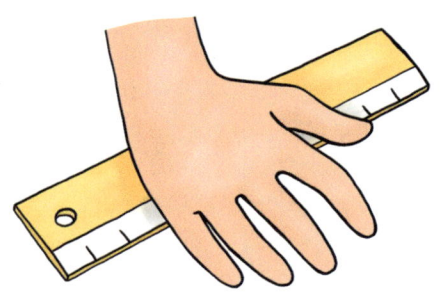

It is a _____ .

It is a _____ .

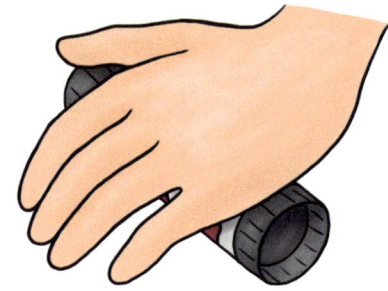

It is a _____ .

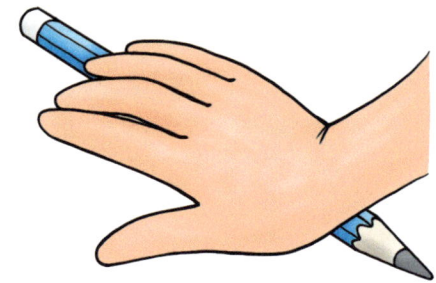

It is a _____ .

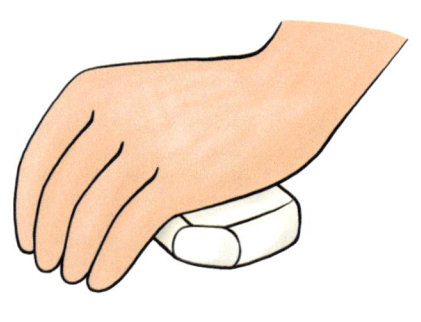

It is a _____ .

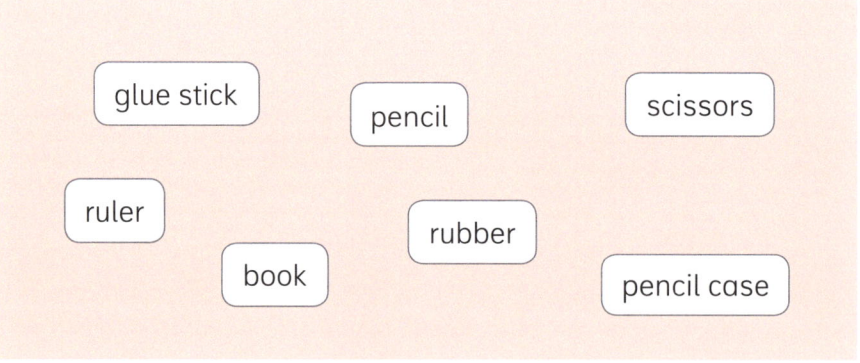

glue stick   pencil   scissors

ruler   rubber

book   pencil case

2 👥 👄 Play the game.

It's a ruler.

What is it?

LET'S PRACTISE!   # Colourful school things

1  Listen and colour the school things.

2 Talk to a partner.

The folder is red.

3 Read and match.

4 Do a colour dictation.

one pen – two pens

three pens

five pencils

four rulers

two rubbers

six glue sticks

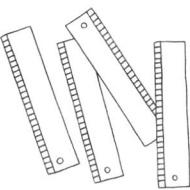

Colour the pens blue.

Shopping lists

1 👁️ ✏️ Read and number the baskets.

1

two glue sticks

a green sharpener

a yellow folder

a red rubber

2

a blue pencil

a red pencil case

two folders

a green rubber

2 ✏️ Write a shopping list for the basket without a number.

Honey page – At school

1 Das sind meine wichtigsten Wörter zum Thema Schule.
Schreibe die Wörter in den Rahmen, die du dir merken möchtest.

Schau nach auf den Seiten 5-8 im TB!

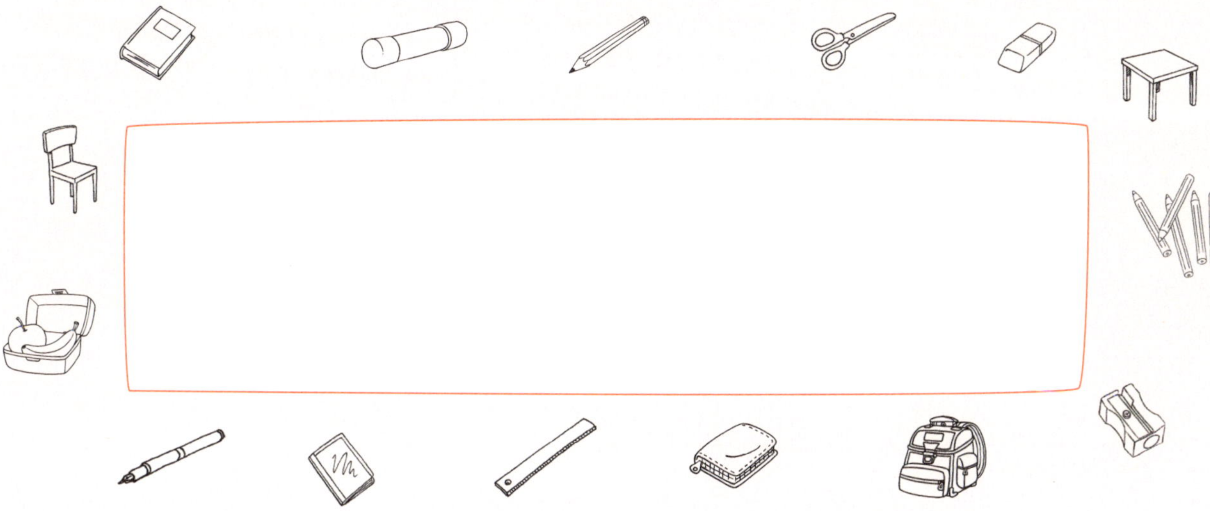

2 Ich kann um einen Schulgegenstand bitten.

Have you got ...?

Yes, I have.
Here you are. /
No, I haven't.

3 Ich kann über mich berichten.

What's your name?	I'm fine/ ...
How old are you?	My name is ...
How are you?	I'm ... years old.

_____

_____

_____

Lisa's new home

1  Find and circle 14 words. (8 → / 6 ↓)

O	B	Q	T	O	I	L	E	T	C	B	G	W	W	A
I	K	V	Y	E	I	M	W	M	Q	L	R	A	E	L
S	G	E	R	P	P	B	A	F	Y	V	A	R	W	J
V	R	X	L	A	M	P	R	O	S	M	N	L	L	K
G	A	R	V	A	E	X	D	B	K	K	D	K	X	T
P	N	H	R	R	B	P	R	A	B	K	F	P	E	A
R	D	Z	S	O	F	A	O	L	I	E	A	H	K	O
B	M	L	W	X	I	G	B	S	I	S	T	E	R	B
P	O	B	N	N	M	S	E	I	W	Z	H	B	K	R
B	T	B	W	K	B	O	O	K	S	H	E	L	F	O
H	H	H	F	R	I	D	G	E	H	U	R	I	Y	T
V	E	M	O	T	H	E	R	T	O	G	V	E	E	H
A	R	K	U	C	X	W	E	T	W	B	E	P	B	E
I	O	S	T	G	F	A	T	H	E	R	L	W	E	R
G	R	H	N	I	W	Y	B	U	R	I	W	M	D	O

Look them up on page 11 in your TB.

2 Write down the words.

family

 _____

 _____

 _____

 _____

 _____

 _____

house

 _____

 _____

 _____

 _____

 toilet

 _____

_____

LET'S PRACTISE! 🗨️ **Find the furniture**

1 🎲 👄 👓 Hide all the furniture. Play the game.

	🚽	💡	🛋️	📚	🧊	🚪	🛏️
kitchen							
hall	Ⓧ						
bedroom							
living room							
bathroom							

Is your toilet in the kitchen?

Is your toilet in the hall?

No, it isn't.

Yes, it is.

2 📖 ✏️ Read and circle the words.

sofatoiletlampbedfridgewardrobebookshelf

3 ✏️ Look at number 1 and complete the sentences.

There is a _____ toilet _____ in the _____ hall _____ .

There is a _____ in the _____ .

There is a _____ in the _____ .

There is a _____ in the _____ .

There is a _____ and a _____ in the _____ .

There is a _____ and a _____ in the _____ .

Lisa's family

1 👂👆 Listen and point.

Mary | William | Monika | Ulrich

Stephanie | Mark

daughter

Lisa | Martin

son

2 📖✏️ Read and circle the words.

grandfatherbrothermotherfathersistersondaughtergrandmother

3 ✏️ Write.

Monika is Lisa's grandmother.   Ulrich is Lisa's _____

_____ is Lisa's brother.   _____ is Lisa's

_____

_____

_____

4 👂📖 Listen, read and check your sentences.

Small families – big families

1  Read, match and fill in the names.

2  Write about the last family.

Park

Wilson

Green

Khan

The **Wilson** family is a big family:
father, mother, two sons and two daughters.
They have got a dog.

The _____ family is
a small family: mother and her son.
They have got a hamster.

The _____ family is
a big family: grandfather, grandmother,
father, mother and a baby daughter.
They have got a cat.

The _____ family is

a big _____ : _____ ,

_____ , _____

and a _____ .

They have got a _____ .

Where is ...?

1  Read the words and match the pictures.

 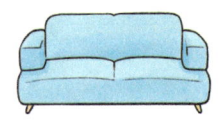    

| sofa | chair | bed | table | wardrobe | lamp |

2 Label the picture.

bed

3 Answer the questions.

Where is the pullover?

The pullover is in the wardrobe.

Where is the teddy bear?

_____

Where is the lamp?

_____

Where is the computer?

_____

Where is the chair?

_____

Where is the football?

_____

Look for help
on page 13 in
your TB.

Honey page – Lisa's new home

1 Das sind meine wichtigsten Wörter zum Thema Räume und Möbel.
Beschrifte alle Gegenstände, an die du dich erinnern kannst.

Schau nach auf den Seiten 10 -13 im TB!

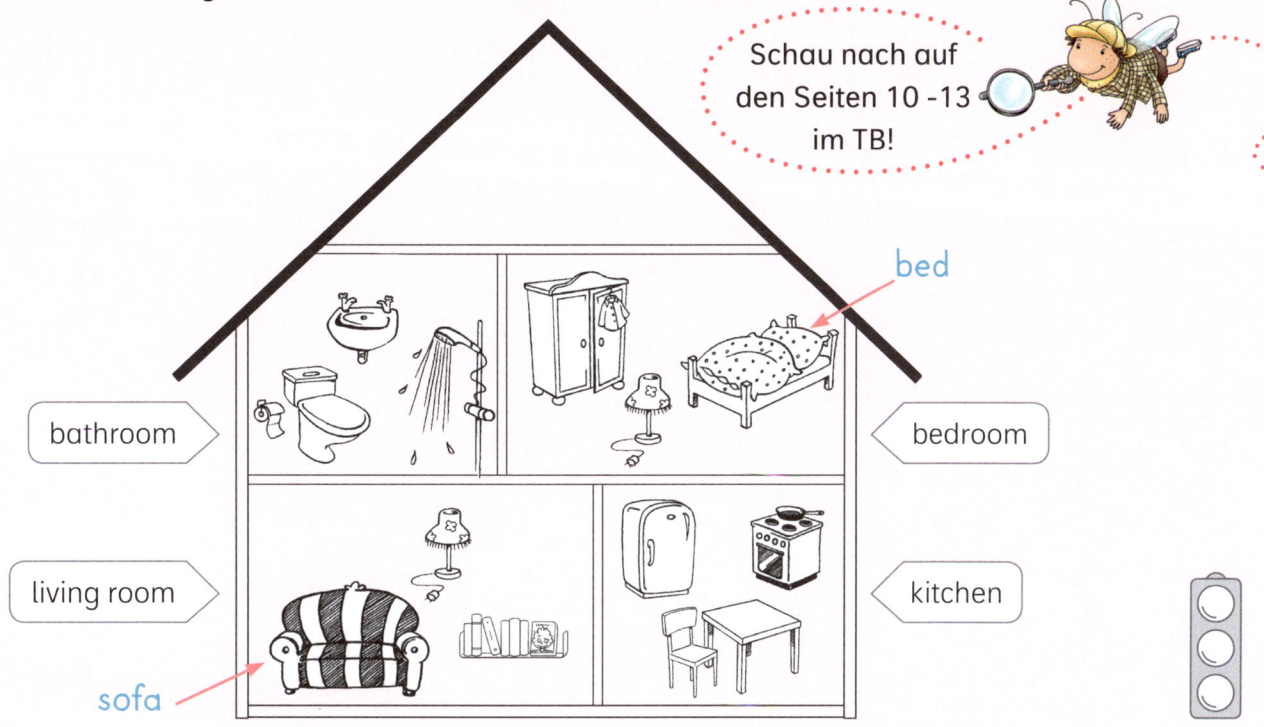

bathroom

bedroom

bed

living room

kitchen

sofa

2 Ich kann sagen, in welchem Zimmer welche Möbel sind.

The _____ is in the _____

_____

_____

_____

3 Ich kann über meine Familie berichten.

Have you got …?

What's your sister's name?

Yes, I've got …/ No, I haven't.

Her name is …

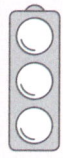

Free time

1 🖉 Do the crossword.

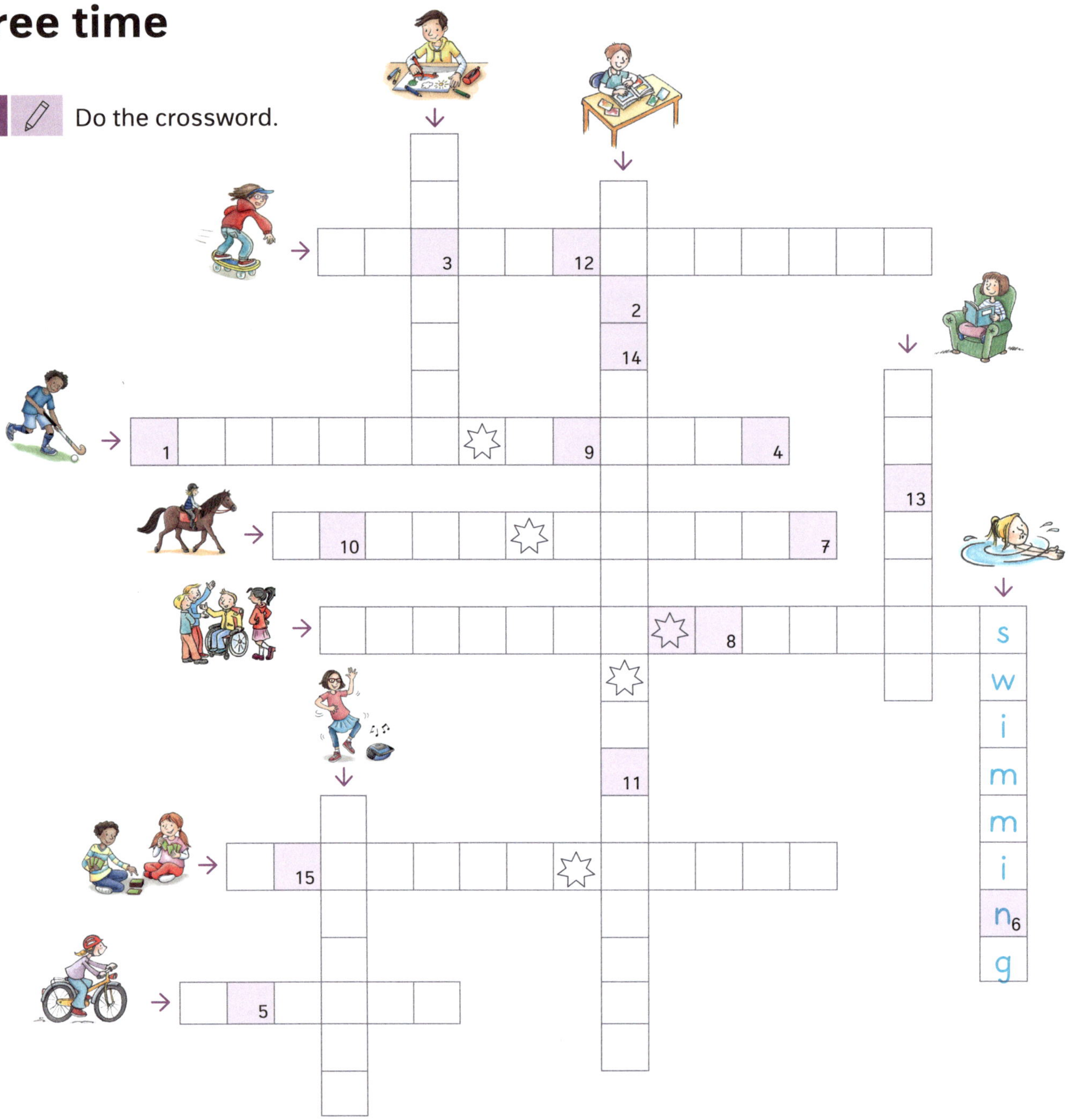

2 🖉 Fill in the missing letters.

1	2	3	4	5	6	7		8	9	10	11	12	13	14	15
					n	☆									

3 🖉 Look at number 2 and complete the sentence.

My favourite hobby is _____ .

Favourite hobbies

1  What are their favourite hobbies? Listen and circle.

Ben

(1. biking)

2. reading

3. drawing

Ben's sister Louise

1. collecting stickers

2. playing
computer games

3. playing football

Ben's father –
Mr Marley

1. meeting friends

2. playing an
instrument

3. taking photos

Ben's mother –
Mrs Marley

1. playing hockey

2. watching films

3. playing tennis

2  Write about Ben's family.

Ben's hobby is biking

His sister's hobby is _____

Ben's father's hobby is _____

His mother's hobby is _____

When can we meet?

1 👂 Listen to the dialogue.

2 👂 📖 Listen and read along.

> When can we meet?

1. Ask a question.

> Let's meet on Friday.

> What can we do?

2. Spin the bottle.

> Let's go skateboarding.

3. Take a Bingo card. Say the sentence.

3 👀 👄 Play the game in a small group. Look here for help.

meet some friends

play football

play tennis

listen to music

go swimming

play cards

dance

play hockey

go skateboarding

go biking

Days of the week

1 🖉 Write in the correct order. Add the short forms.

Saturday	Monday	MON
~~Monday~~		
Thursday		
Sunday		
Wednesday		
Friday		
Tuesday		

TUE
FRI
~~MON~~
THU
SAT
SUN
WED

2 📖 🖉 Read and match.

Hello, I'm Lucy. My favourite hobby is skateboarding. On Wednesday I go skateboarding with my friends. There is a skate park near my school.

THU

WED

My name is Shan. My hobbies are playing table tennis and swimming. On Thursday I go swimming with Dad. Every Sunday we play table tennis in the garden.

SUN

TUE

FRI

My name is Meena. My hobbies are biking and horse riding. On Tuesday I go biking with my friends. On Friday I go horse riding on a farm.

SAT

MON

Aufgabe 2: Zwei Wochentagsabkürzungen bleiben übrig.

My busy week

1   Read the words.

2   Colour the days green and the activities red.

Thursday

play football

go biking

Monday

go swimming

Sunday

play computer games

Wednesday

Tuesday

go horse riding

meet friends

play table tennis

Saturday

play basketball

play hockey

go shopping with Grandma

Friday

3   What do you do during the week? Tell your partner.

4   Write about **your** week.

On Monday I go shopping with Grandma.

Honey page – Free time

1 Das sind meine wichtigsten Wörter zum Thema Hobbies. Schreibe die Wörter in den Rahmen, die du dir merken möchtest.

Schau nach auf den Seiten 19 und 23 im TB!

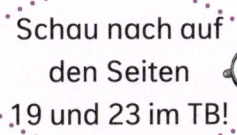

swimming,

2 Ich kann meine Lieblingshobbys aufzählen.

My favourite hobbies are _____

_____

3 Ich kann mich mit jemandem verabreden.

1 Can we meet on Monday?

2 Sorry, on Monday I go swimming.

3 What about Tuesday?

4 Okay, let's play table tennis on Tuesday.

1 Can we _____

2 _____

3 _____

4 _____

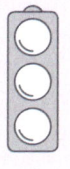

Pets

1 👂 ✏️ Listen and tick the correct word.

○ goldfish ○ cat 	○ mice ○ hamsters	○ mouse ○ cat
○ rabbit ○ cat	○ mice ○ guinea pigs	○ dog ○ guinea pig
○ cat ○ dog ○ hamster	○ dog ○ guinea pig ○ rabbit	○ budgie ○ mouse ○ rabbit

2 📖 ✏️ Find the pets and circle them. (6 → / 4 ↓)

3 ✏️ Write.

G	A	B	U	D	G	I	E	R	K	D
O	B	G	M	Q	U	H	A	E	L	O
L	G	U	I	N	E	A	☆	P	I	G
D	C	H	N	R	K	M	B	F	M	O
F	D	I	M	O	U	S	E	G	C	P
I	R	A	B	B	I	T	H	C	A	R
S	E	H	O	S	V	E	D	I	T	S
H	F	M	I	C	E	R	A	T	H	T

guinea pig

_____

_____

_____

_____

_____

_____

_____

_____

_____

  **What's your favourite pet?**

1 👁️👂👄✏️ Do a class survey.

What's your favourite pet?

My favourite pet is a cat.

	dog	cat	rabbit	guinea pig	hamster	mouse	budgie	goldfish	rat		
Mia		X									

2 👁️👂👄✏️ Find the most popular pets in your class.

1. _____

2. _____

3. _____

Pets in class

1  Listen and number.

2  Listen and check.

3 Read and fill in the missing words.

| mice | ~~tail~~ | ~~grey~~ | ~~long~~ | ~~legs~~ | cat food | ~~four~~ |

The cat is grey. It has got four legs and a long tail.

It sleeps in a basket. It likes _____ and _____.

| carrots | legs | tail | yellow | short | cage |

The hamster is _____. It has got four _____ and a _____

_____. It lives in a _____. It likes _____.

| four | basket | brown | bones | dog | white | long |

The _____ is _____ and _____.

It has got _____ legs and a _____ tail. It sleeps in a _____.

It likes _____ and dog food.

| fish food | orange | fish bowl | legs |

The goldfish is _____. It has got no _____. It lives in a

_____. It likes _____.

The rabbit and the goldfish

1 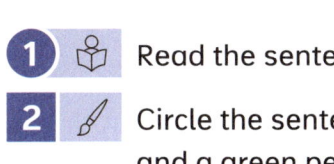 Read the sentences.

2 Circle the sentences. Take a red pencil for the rabbit and a green pencil for the goldfish.

My pet has got four legs.

My pet eats fish flakes.

My pet lives in a big cage.

My pet has got two long ears.

My pet lives in a fish bowl.

My pet is orange.

My pet eats grains.

My pet can run.

My pet can swim.

My pet has got no legs.

fish bowl

fish flakes

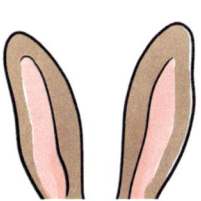

long ears

3 Write about the rabbit or the goldfish. Copy the sentences.

_____

_____

_____

_____

_____

All about my favourite pet

Look for help on pages 26 and 27 in your TB.

1 ✏️ What can you say about your favourte pet? Collect words.

Colour: It is …

brown, _____

_____

Body parts: It has got ….

a head, _____

_____

Food: It likes …

water, _____

_____

Home: It lives in …

a cage, _____

_____

Special facts: It can…

run, _____

_____

2 ✏️ Write about your favourte pet.

All about my favourite pet

_____

_____

_____

_____

_____

3 👄 Present your favourite pet in class.

This is my favourite pet.

Aufgabe 1: SuS sammeln Wörter auf einem Extrablatt.

Honey page – Pets

1 Das sind meine wichtigsten Wörter zum Thema Haustiere.
Schreibe die Wörter in den Rahmen, die du dir merken möchtest.

Schau nach auf den Seiten 25-27 im TB!

2 Ich kann meine Lieblingshaustiere aufzählen.

I like _____.

My favourite pet is a _____.

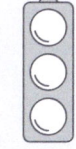

3 Ich kann mich über Haustiere unterhalten.

I've got a hamster. A hamster eats …

I've got a budgie. A budgie drinks …

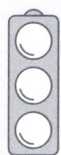

At the shopping centre

 **1** What's wrong? Circle.

 **2** Write the four words.

Look for help on page 33 in your TB.

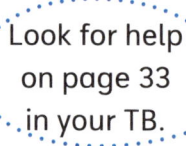

3 Read and circle the odd one out.

> 1. raincoat - dress - take off - skirt - trousers - shoes
>
> 2. laptop - bananas - butter - pears - cheese - carrots
>
> 3. budgie - hamster - rabbit - mouse - dress - cat

4 Write your own odd one out. Swap with your partner.

Shopping

1 Read the words.

2  Match the words with the right shops. Write them down.

bananas	skirt	carrots	cheese	raincoat	~~bread~~
trousers	cereals	shoes	pineapples	jeans	apples
butter	dress	pears	T-shirt	cornflakes	cap

bread

3 Label.

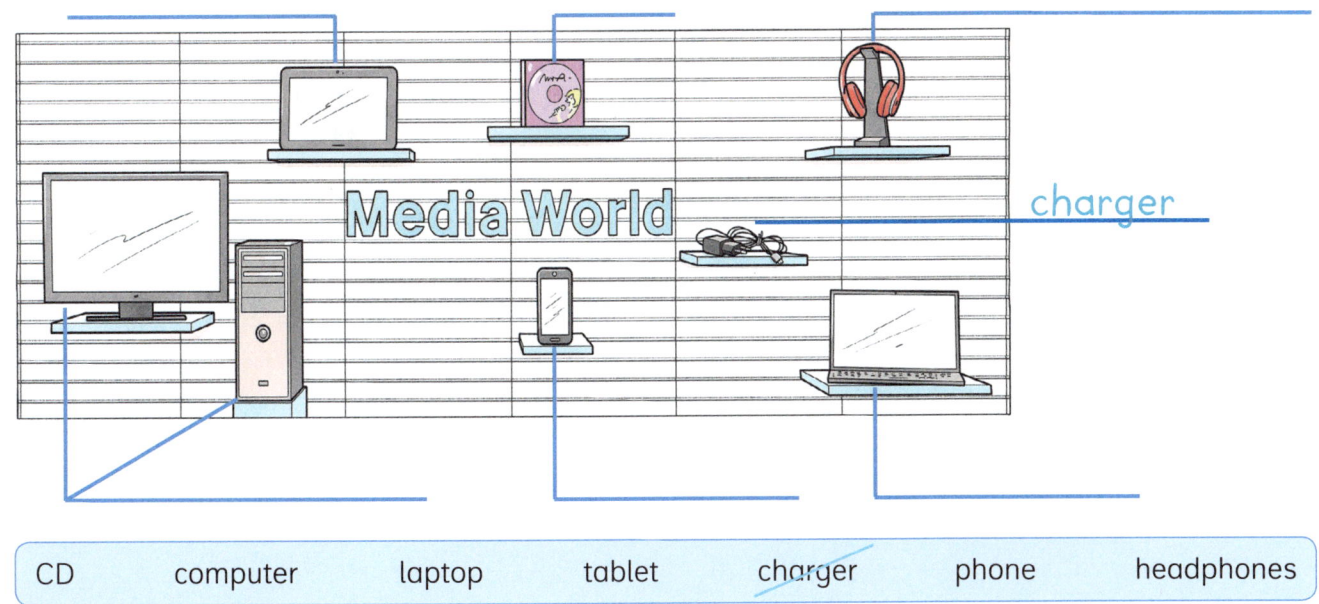

charger

Media World

| CD | computer | laptop | tablet | charger | phone | headphones |

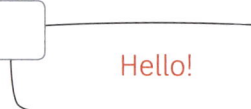
Shopping dialogue

1. 👂 Listen.
2. 👂 📖 ✏️ Listen again. Read along and number the speech bubbles in the right order (1-9).
3. 👀👂 👄 Practise the dialogue.
4. 👀 👀👂 👄 Act out your own role play.

Hello!

Hm, I don't like them. What about the red T-shirt? How much is it?

Bye!

I'd like to buy a pair of shoes.

Hello! Can I help you?

Thank you. Goodbye!

It's 2 pounds.

Okay! Here you are.

Look here are some nice sports shoes.

No T-shirt for Cameron?

1 👂 Listen to the story again.

2 📖 ✏️ Read the sentences and tick the right words.

3 👀 👄 Check with your partner.

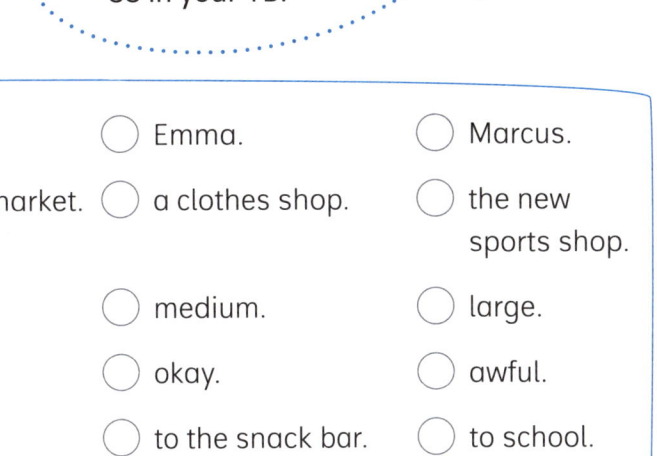

Look for help on page 35 in your TB.

1. Cameron talks to	◯ Ben.	◯ Emma.	◯ Marcus.
2. They go to	◯ the supermarket.	◯ a clothes shop.	◯ the new sports shop.
3. Cameron's size is	◯ small.	◯ medium.	◯ large.
4. Cameron thinks orange is	◯ great.	◯ okay.	◯ awful.
5. His friend wants to go	◯ home.	◯ to the snack bar.	◯ to school.
6. Cameron's favourite colour is	◯ pink.	◯ green.	◯ blue.
7. On his T-shirt there is	◯ a spaceship.	◯ a dinosaur.	◯ a football.
8. The new T-shirt is	◯ 6 pounds.	◯ 8 pounds.	◯ 5 pounds.

4 👂 ✏️ Listen to the end of the story. Tick the correct picture.

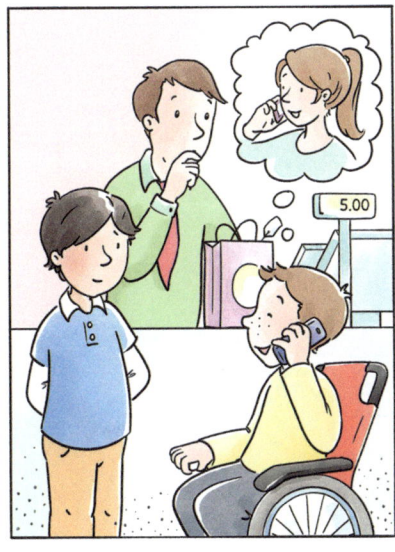

◯

◯

◯

Breakfast with Ben's family

1  Listen to the chant.

2 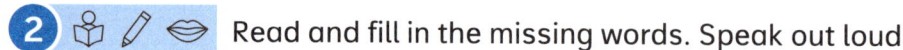 Read and fill in the missing words. Speak out loud.

3 Mark the keywords.

Ben is at the table.

Jam is on his plate.

Now it's time for breakfast.

He isn't late.

Mum is at the table.

Cheese is on her plate.

Now it's time for breakfast.

She isn't late.

Dad is at the table.

_____ is on _____ plate.

Now it's time for breakfast.

He _____ late.

isn't = is not

4 Write your own chant. Present it.

Honey page – At the shopping centre

1 Das sind meine wichtigsten Wörter zum Thema Einkaufen.
Schreibe die Wörter in den Rahmen, die du dir merken möchtest.

Schau nach auf den Seiten 33 und 34 im TB!

2 Ich kann über mein Lieblingseis berichten und es bestellen.

What's your favourite ice cream? - My favourite ice cream is

_____ .

What can I do for you? - I'd like _____ scoop(s) of

_____ in a cone, please.

3 Ich kann fragen wieviel etwas kostet.

How much is/are ... ?

That's ... pounds.

A trip to London

🌍 🎲 👄 Play the game.

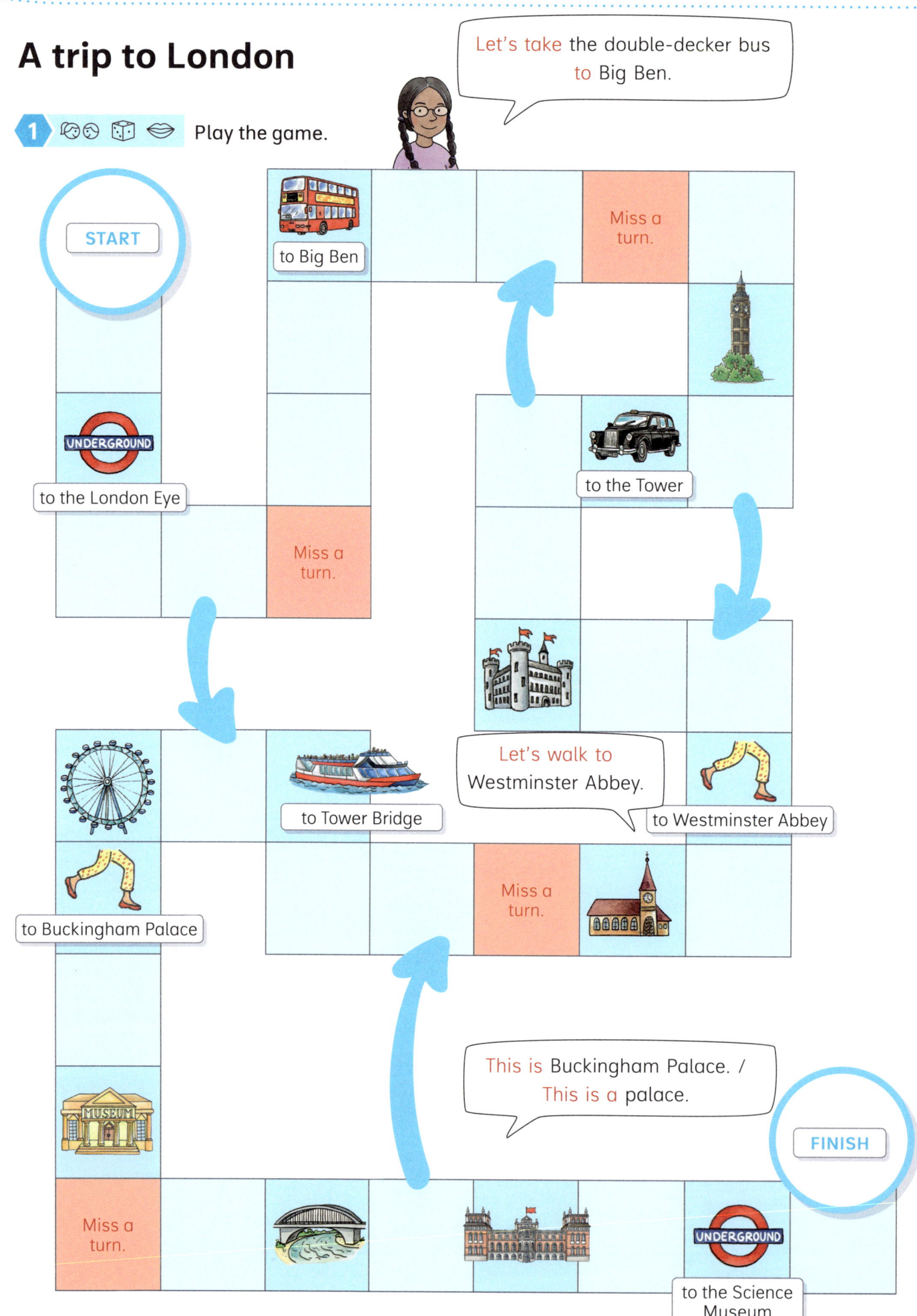

Let's take the double-decker bus to Big Ben.

START

to Big Ben

Miss a turn.

UNDERGROUND
to the London Eye

Miss a turn.

to the Tower

Let's walk to Westminster Abbey.

to Tower Bridge

to Westminster Abbey

to Buckingham Palace

Miss a turn.

This is Buckingham Palace. / This is a palace.

FINISH

MUSEUM

Miss a turn.

UNDERGROUND
to the Science Museum

A visit from Scotland

Look for help on page 38 in your TB.

1 Read and tick the right words.

1. Emma's cousin is coming to London. His name is …
   - ◯ Paul.   S
   - ◯ Anna.   L
   - ◯ David.   R

2. Her cousin and his family are coming for …
   - ◯ three days.   E
   - ◯ a week.   O
   - ◯ a weekend.   A

3. They are coming …
   - ◯ on the underground.   U
   - ◯ by taxi.   F
   - ◯ by train.   C

4. On a sunny day Mrs Brown would like to go to …
   - ◯ Big Ben.   B
   - ◯ Hyde Park.   K
   - ◯ London Zoo.   W

5. Mike would like to visit the …
   - ◯ Science Museum.   E
   - ◯ Tower.   J
   - ◯ London Eye.   Z

6. Emma would like to go …
   - ◯ on a bus trip.   P
   - ◯ on a boat trip.   T
   - ◯ on a train journey.   V

2  Fill in the letters from sentences 1–6. Write the solution.

1	2	3	4	5	6

Mike wants to show David the ___ ___ ___ ___ ___ ___ in the Science Museum.

What would you like to do in Hyde Park?

1 👂 ✏️ Listen and number.

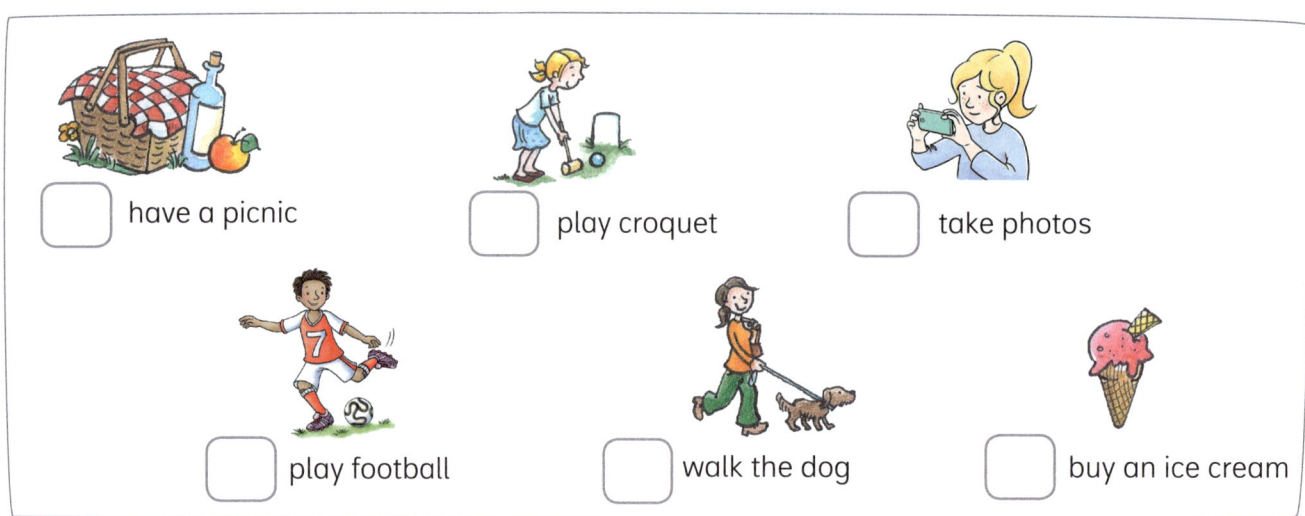

☐ have a picnic

☐ play croquet

☐ take photos

☐ play football

☐ walk the dog

☐ buy an ice cream

2 👂 Listen to the dialogue.

I'd like to take photos. How about you?

What would you like to do in Hyde Park?

I'd like to have a picnic.

3 👀 👄 ✏️ Ask three children.

name	🧺	⚽	🏑	🐕	📷	🍦
_____						
_____						
_____						

The London Eye

1  Listen and read along.

LONDON EYE

It is 120 metres in diameter.

The London Eye is the biggest ferris wheel in Europe.

It was built in 1999.

It is 135 metres high.

The London Eye has 32 capsules.

25 people fit in one capsule. One round in the London Eye takes 30 minutes.

---

2   Read the questions and answer.

Es ist 135 m hoch.

Wie hoch ist das London Eye?

Wann wurde es gebaut?

Was ist das London Eye?	
Wann wurde es gebaut?	
Wie hoch ist das London Eye?	
Wie groß ist der Durchmesser?	
Wie viele Gondeln hat das London Eye?	
Wie viele Personen passen in eine Gondel?	
Wie lange dauert eine Umdrehung im London Eye?	

3  Check with a partner.

A postcard

1   Read the postcard.

Dear Ian,
London is great!
The weather is sunny.
My cousin Emma and I are on
a sightseeing tour today.
I like Tower Bridge, Big Ben
and the London Eye best.
It's really cool!

See you, David

Ian Stafford

5, Palmerston Road

Dublin 14

Republic of Ireland

2 Read the postcard again and tick David's favourite sights.

◯ ◯ ◯ ◯ ◯ ◯

3 Write your own postcard.

Dear _____,

London is _____!

The weather is _____.

My _____

and I are on a sightseeing tour today.

I like _____.

_____ best.

It's really _____!

See you, _____

_____

_____

_____

London is...
great • exciting •
interesting • cool ...

The weather is...
rainy • foggy •
windy ...

My ...
cousin • friend •
brother • sister ...

It's really...
great • exciting •
interesting • cool ...

Honey page – A trip to London

1 Das sind meine wichtigsten Wörter zum Thema London.
Schreibe die Wörter in den Rahmen, die du dir merken möchtest.

Schau nach auf den Seiten 39-42 im TB!

2 Ich kann einige Sehenswürdigkeiten erklären.

_____ is the palace of the royal family.

_____ is a bridge over the River Thames.

_____ is a big ferris wheel.

_____ is a museum showing the Crown Jewels.

3 Ich kann mich darüber unterhalten, was man in London machen kann.

What would you like to do in London?

I'd like to see Big Ben.

I'd like to visit _____

I'd like to _____

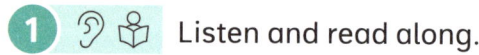
What's the weather like?

1 🦻 📦 Listen and read along.

What's the weather like in Glasgow in spring?

It's rainy in Glasgow.

Look for help on page 47 in your TB!

2 👀 🖌️ 👄 Complete the weather maps. Talk to your partner.

spring

summer

autumn

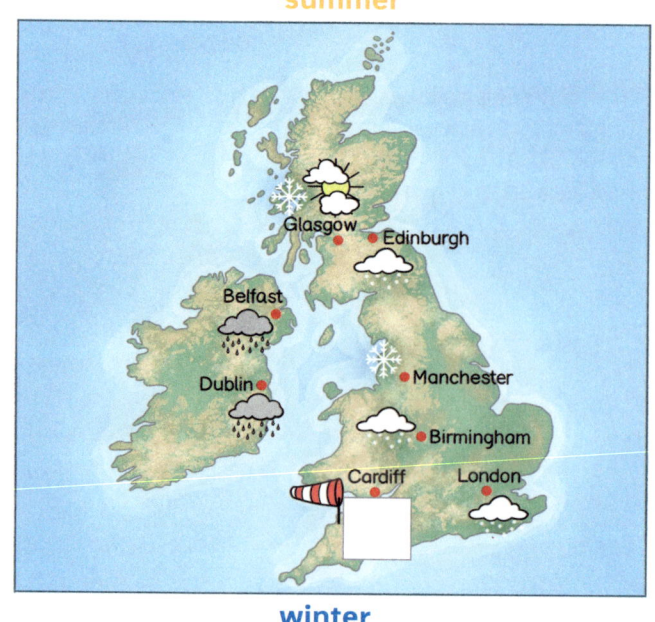

winter

Emma's birthday party

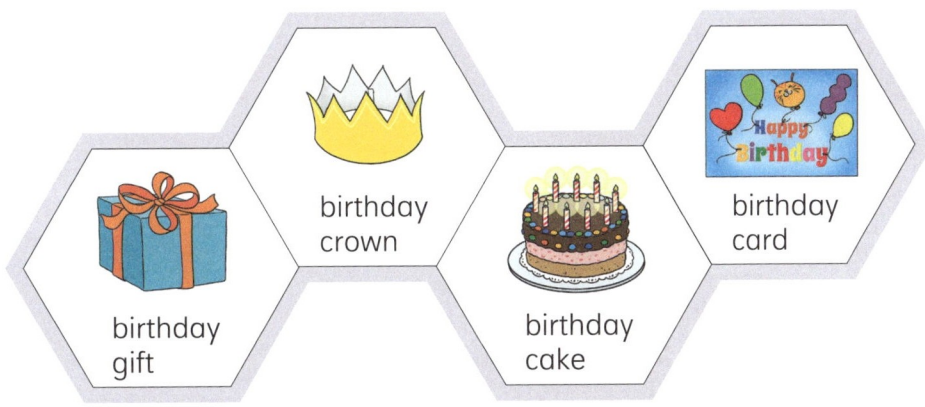

birthday crown

birthday gift

birthday cake

birthday card

Pupil's Audio-CD 35

1 👂✋ Listen and point.

2 📖✏ Read the sentences. Are they true or false? Tick.

3 👀✏👄 Write more true or false sentences. Check with your partner.

	😊	🙁
There are six muffins on the table.		
There is a pink birthday cake.		
Emma's friends eat cucumbers.		
There are three gifts on the table.		
Lisa and Ben have a nice birthday card for Emma.		

Halloween: A ghost story

1 👂 👆 Listen and point.

2 👄 What is the story about? Talk about it in German.

3 🖌 Finish the last picture.

CD 84
SC 35–40
Fö/Fo 33

Decorate a Christmas tree

1 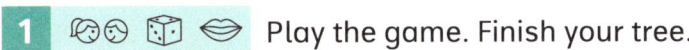 Play the game. Finish your tree.

> Roll your dice. What have you got?

> I've got a four. So I draw a candle for my Christmas tree.

angel	star	bell	candle	reindeer	bauble
⚀	⚁	⚂	⚃	⚄	⚅

2 Talk about your Christmas trees.

> On my Christmas tree I've got …

Sechsmal würfeln. Das gewürfelte Schmuckstück in den Baum zeichnen.
Den eigenen Baum vorstellen.

KV 81
Fö/Fo 34

forty-three / **43**

How to make pancakes

1  Listen and point.

2 Listen again. Number the pictures.

Easter partner dictation

1 🖌 Draw 6 coloured Easter eggs in picture **A**.

2 👁👁 👄 Tell your partner where your Easter eggs are. Your partner has to draw them into picture **B**.

> There is a red Easter egg under the bench.

A

B

Numbers 1

1 👂 👄 Listen and repeat.

Pupil's Audio-CD 41

11 eleven
12 twelve
13 thirteen
14 fourteen
15 fifteen
16 sixteen
17 seventeen
18 eighteen
19 nineteen

2 👂 🖌 Listen and draw.

3 👀 👄 🖌 Do a colour dictation. Colour the numbers of the houses.

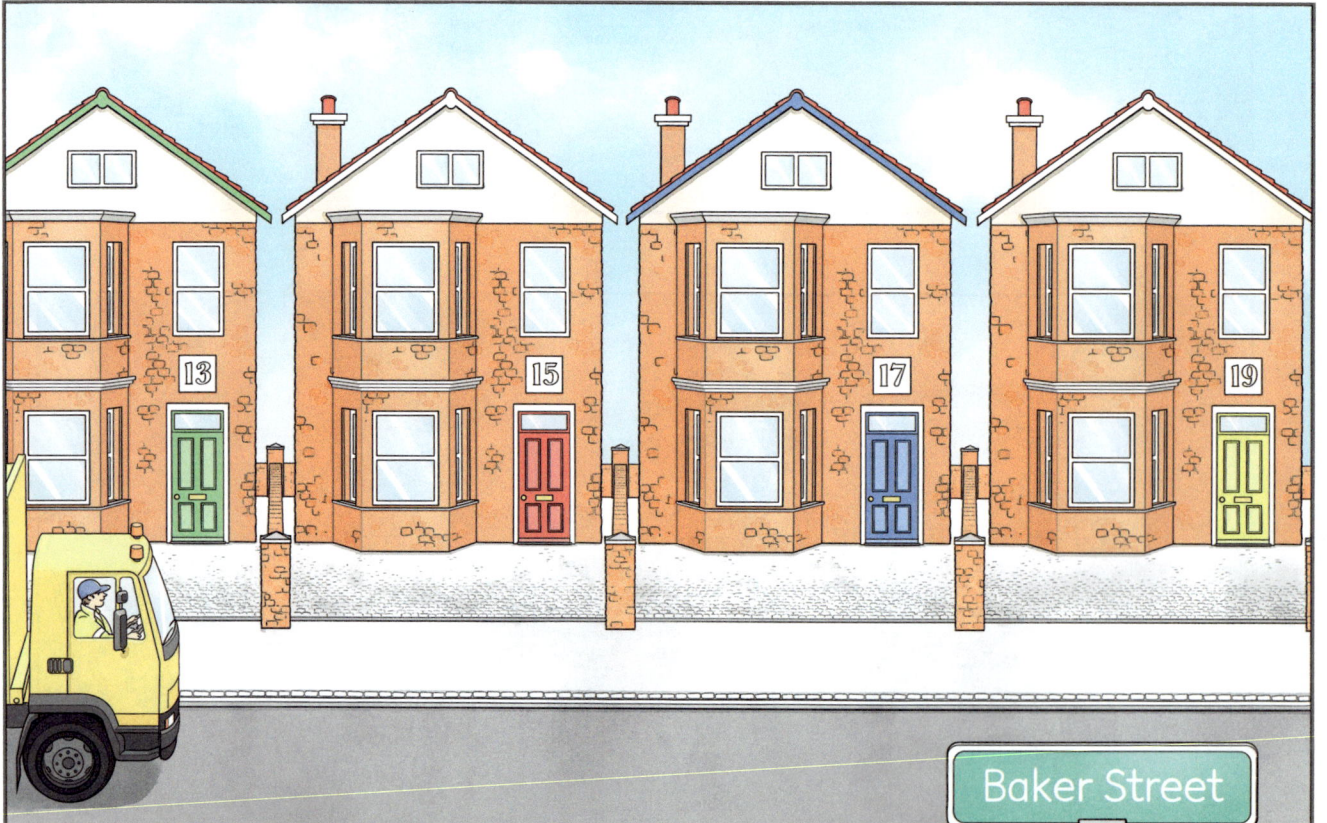

CD 95-96
FC/WC 41-42, 249-255
KV 86
Fö/Fo 37

Numbers 2

1 👂 👄 Listen and repeat.

Pupil's Audio-CD 42

2 ✏️ Write the missing numbers.

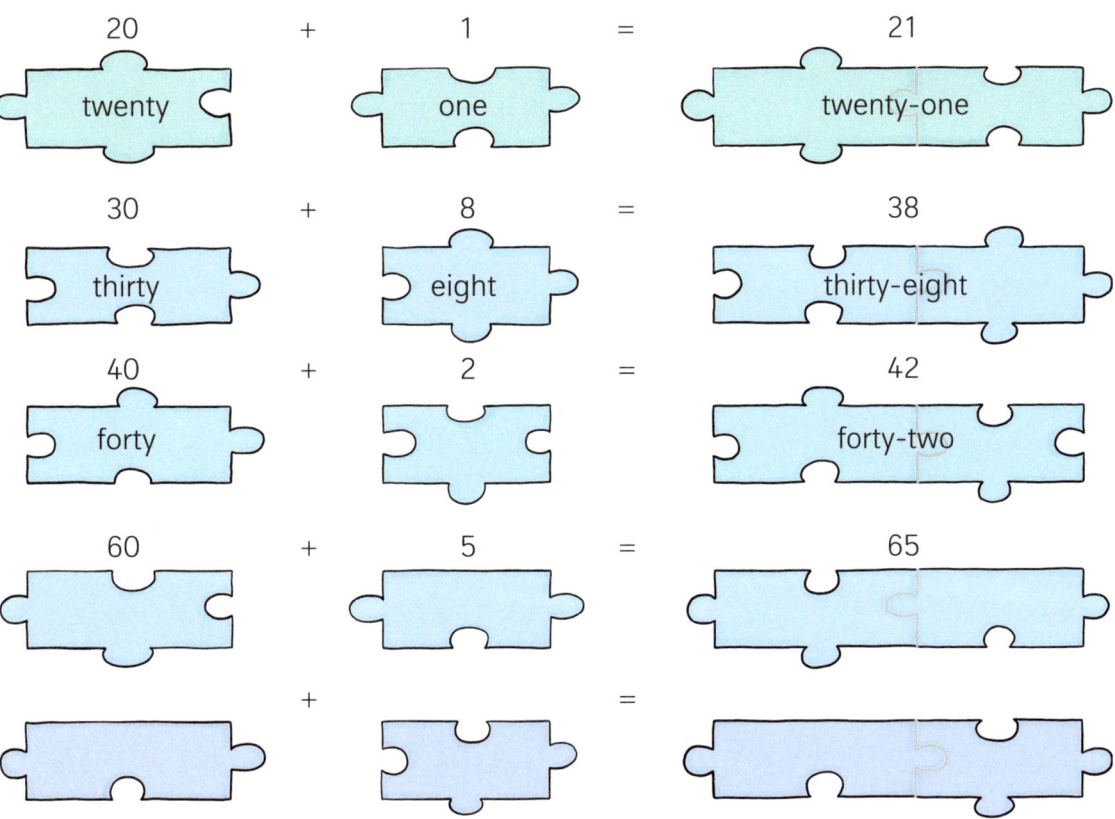

20	+	1	=	21
twenty		one		twenty-one

30	+	8	=	38
thirty		eight		thirty-eight

40	+	2	=	42
forty				forty-two

60	+	5	=	65

| + | = |

3 👂 ✏️ Listen and write the numbers. ___ ___ ___ ___ ___

Fit for 4!

1 🎲 ✏️ Look at picture ☐1 on page 54 in your textbook. Read the questions and fill in one word from your answer into the crossword.

Across →
1 What are the boys playing?
2 What season is it?
3 What animals are swimming in the pond?
4 Where are all the people?
5 What are the man and the woman doing?

Down ↓
1 What are the children taking for a walk?
2 Where are the goldfish?
3 What can you buy at the candy van?
4 What are the football players wearing?
5 How many boys are playing football?

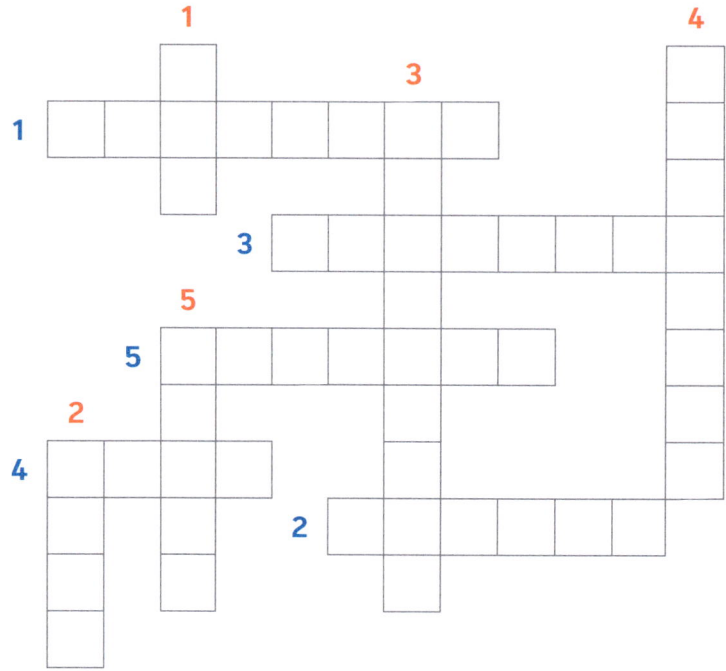

2 🎲 ✏️ Read and number.

3 👀 👄 ✏️ Look at picture ☐2 on page 54 in your textbook. Do a colour dictation.

1 A place where you can buy ice cream.

2 Two people are playing with boats.

3 A person is on inline skates.

4 Two people are lying in the sun.

5 Five baby ducks are swimming in the pond.

6 Something that is wrong in the picture.

KV 90-92
Fö/Fo 39

Fit for 4!

1 📖 ✏️ Look at picture 3 on page 55 in your textbook. Read and find the matching answer.

1	What season is it?	**d**	At the stall.
2	Who is flying the wonderful kites?	**y**	The Easter nest
3	What colour are the horses?	**a**	There are three ducks.
4	Where can you buy sandwiches?	**w**	It's autumn.
5	Who is just buying a cheese sandwich?	**n**	They are brown.
6	What is the family feeding?	**i**	Two children.
7	How many ducks are there in the pond?	**y**	An old lady.
8	What is wrong in this picture?	**d**	The ducks in the pond.

2 ✏️ Write the solution.

1	2	3	4	5

6	7	8

It's a

3 📖 ✏️ Look at picture 4 on page 55 in your textbook. Read the sentences and circle the wrong words.

1. It is a cold day in summer.
2. You can buy cold drinks at the stall.
3. One boy is playing ice hockey on the pond.
4. One child is making an Easter man.
5. Three children are having a strawberry fight.
6. A man and a little girl are coming back from a shopping tour.

4 ✏️ Do you know the correct words? Write three correct sentences.

The correct sentences

Classroom phrases

My words

Look up numbers 13–100 on pages 46 and 47 in your WB!

colours

red ...... (red)
orange .... (orange)
yellow .... (yellow)
green ..... (green)
blue ...... (blue)
purple .... (purple)

pink .... (pink)
brown .... (brown)
white ..... (white)
black ..... (black)
grey ...... (grey)

_____

_____

numbers

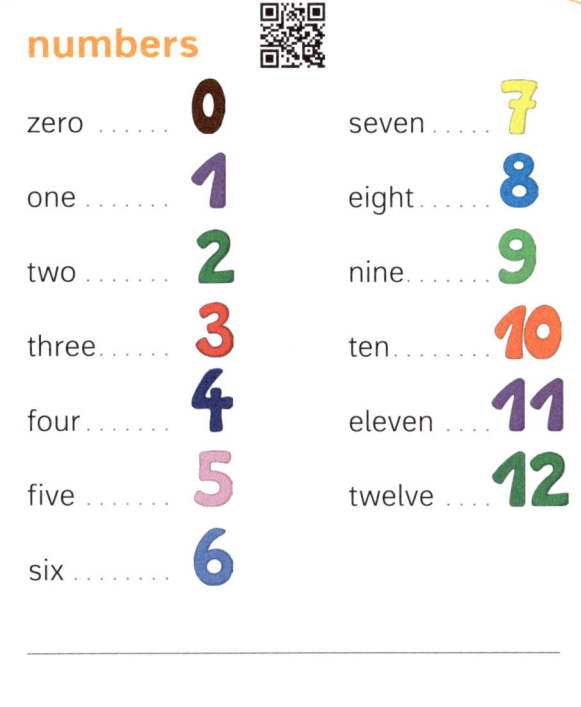

zero 0
one 1
two 2
three 3
four 4
five 5
six 6

seven 7
eight 8
nine 9
ten 10
eleven 11
twelve 12

_____

_____

feelings

fine .... (fine)
happy ..... (happy)

sad .... (sad)
tired ...... (tired)

_____

school things

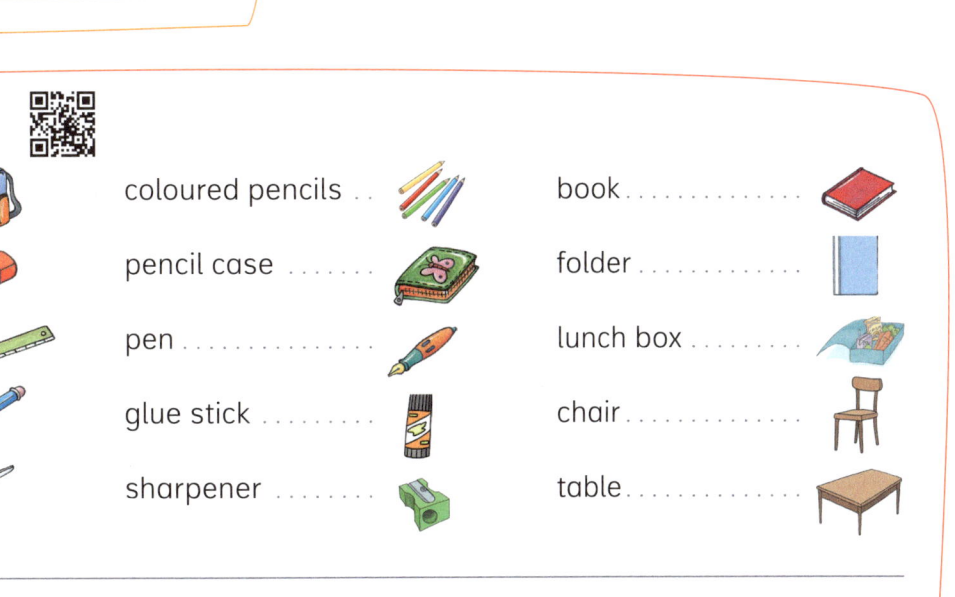

school bag .... (school bag)
rubber .... (rubber)
ruler .... (ruler)
pencil .... (pencil)
scissors .... (scissors)

coloured pencils .. (coloured pencils)
pencil case .... (pencil case)
pen .... (pen)
glue stick .... (glue stick)
sharpener .... (sharpener)

book .... (book)
folder .... (folder)
lunch box .... (lunch box)
chair .... (chair)
table .... (table)

_____

_____

rooms and furniture

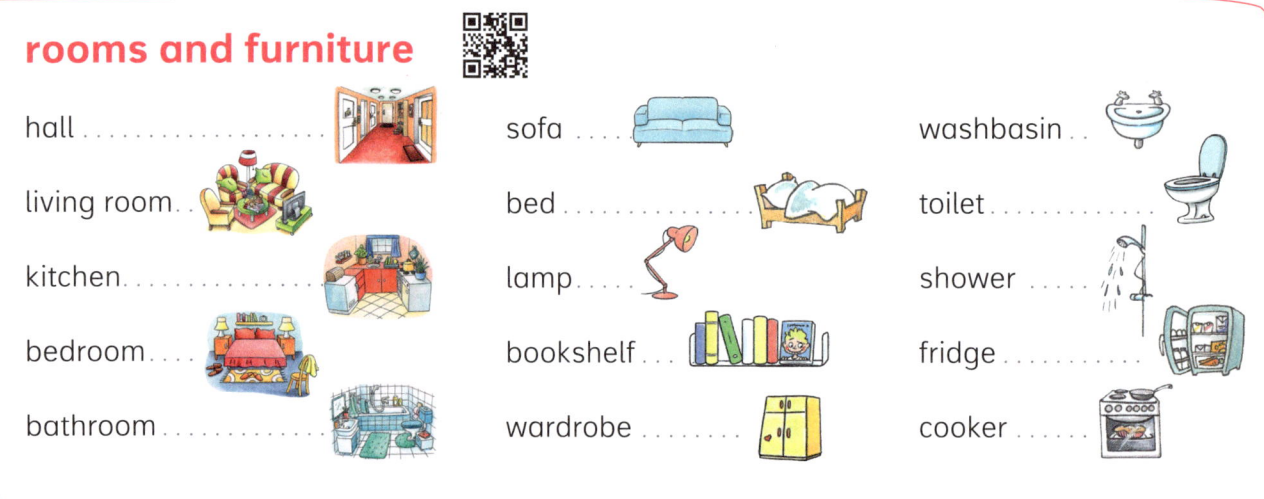

hall . . . .

living room . .

kitchen . . . .

bedroom . . . .

bathroom . . . .

sofa . . . .

bed . . . .

lamp . . . .

bookshelf . . . .

wardrobe . . . .

washbasin . .

toilet . . . .

shower . . . . .

fridge . . . . . .

cooker . . . .

_____

family

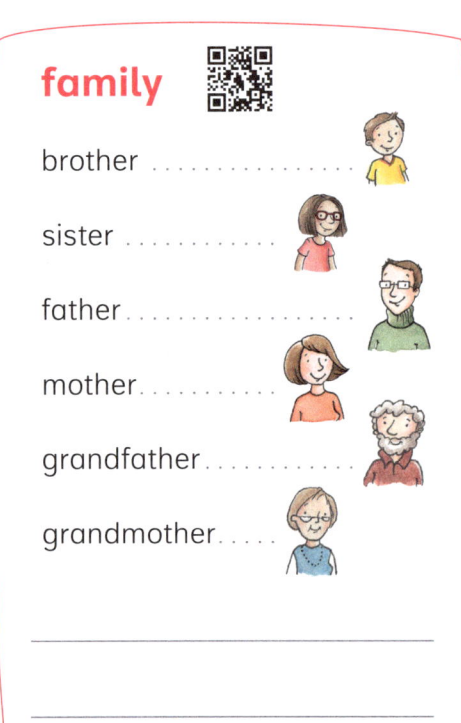

brother . . . .

sister . . . .

father . . . .

mother . . . .

grandfather . . . .

grandmother . . . . .

_____

_____

prepositions

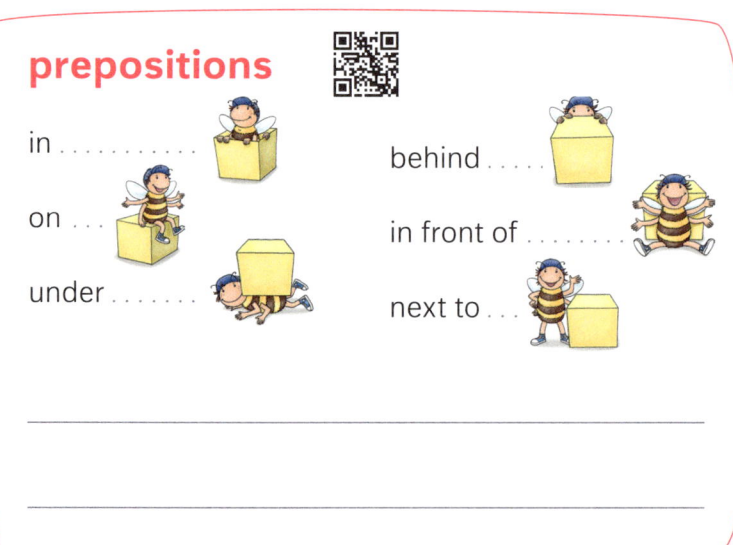

in . . . .

on . . .

under . . . .

behind . . . . .

in front of . . . .

next to . . .

_____

_____

feelings

proud . . . .

angry . . . . . .

excited . . . . . .

_____

_____

days of the week

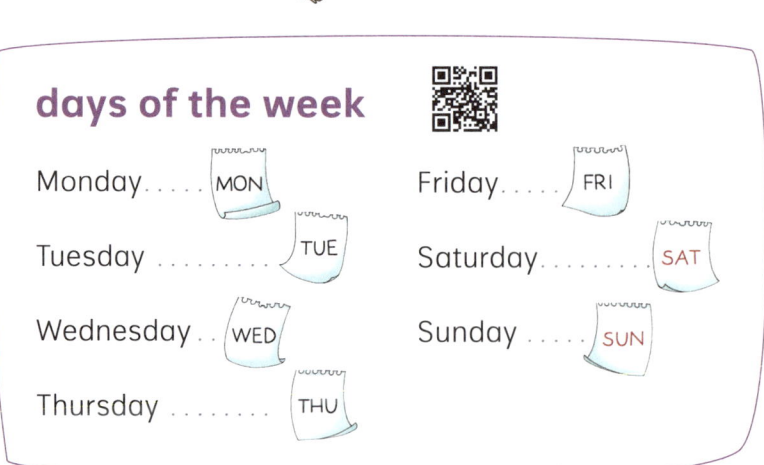

Monday . . . . MON

Tuesday . . . . TUE

Wednesday . . WED

Thursday . . . . THU

Friday . . . . . FRI

Saturday . . . . SAT

Sunday . . . . . SUN

Diff ▲ L kann zusätzlich zum Einsatz von Bildwörterbüchern oder Online-Wörterbüchern anregen.

hobbies

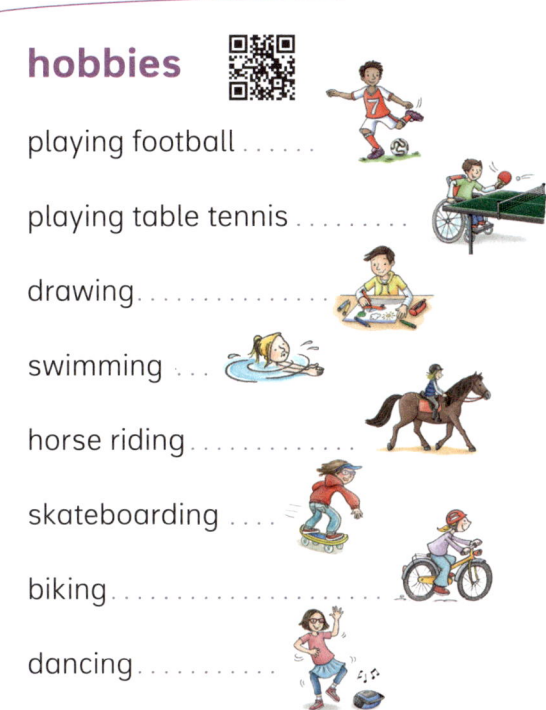

playing football . . . . . .

playing table tennis . . . .

drawing. . . . .

swimming . . .

horse riding. . . . .

skateboarding . . . .

biking. . . . .

dancing. . . . .

playing computer games. . . .

reading . . . .

playing an instrument . . . . .

collecting stickers . . .

playing hockey . . . .

playing cards . . . . . .

meeting friends . . . .

pets and body parts

dog . . . . . .

cat. . . . .

mouse . . . . .

mice . . . .

hamster . . . .

rabbit . . . .

goldfish . . . . .

guinea pig . . . . . .

budgie . . . . . .

rat . . . .

mouth . . . . . .

nose . . . .

eyes . . . .

ears . . . .

legs. . . . .

tail. . . . .

pet food

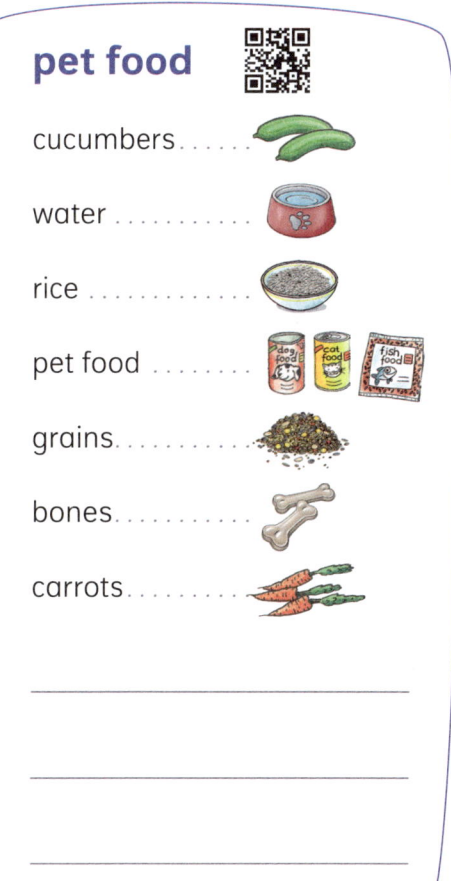

cucumbers. . . . . .

water . . . .

rice . . . .

pet food . . . .

grains. . . . .

bones. . . . .

carrots. . . . .

clothes

skirt ....

trousers ..

dress ....

raincoat ....

shoes ....

put on ......

take off ....

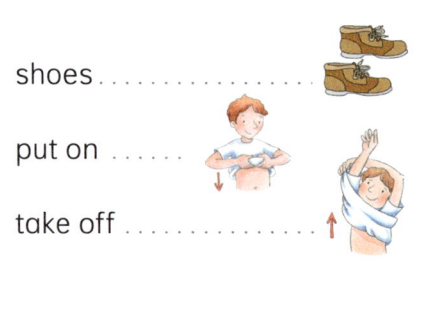

_____

_____

food

cheese ....

jam ....

bread ....

butter ....

cereals ....

bacon and eggs ..

apple ....

pear ....

pineapple ....

vanilla ice cream

chocolate ice cream ....

strawberry ice cream ....

hazelnut ice cream

cherry ice cream ..

lemon ice cream

kiwi ice cream .....

blue angel ice cream ....

_____

_____

media

CD ....

computer ...

laptop ......

tablet ......

phone ....

charger ....

headphones .....

_____

English money

pounds ....

pence ......

_____

_____

sights, transport and activities

palace . . . .

church . . . .

bridge . . . .

ferris wheel . . . . . .

castle . . . .

museum . . . .

underground . . . .

taxi . . . .

double-decker bus . . . .

train . . . .

boat . . . .

walk . . . .

take a photo . . . . .

visit . . . .

see . . . .

seasons and weather

spring . . . .

summer . . . . .

autumn . . . .

winter . . . . . .

frosty . . . .

snowy . . . . . .

cloudy . . . . . .

rainy . . . . . .

warm . . . .

sunny . . . .

hot . . . .

thundery . . . .

cold . . . .

foggy . . . .

windy . . . .

Special days

birthday

birthday gift . . . . . .

birthday crown . . . .

birthday cake . . . . .

birthday card . . . . .

_____

_____

Halloween

ghost . . . . .

pumpkin . .

bat . . . .

skeleton . .

spider . . . . .

vampire . . .

witch . . . . .

Christmas

Christmas tree . .

Father Christmas .

angel . . . .

star . . . .

bell . . . .

candle . . . .

reindeer . . . .

bauble . . . .

Christmas stocking

Easter

Easter egg . . . .

Easter basket

Easter bunny . . . .

bush . . . . .

tree . . . . . .

bench . . . . . .

Bumblebee

Workbook für Englisch in Klasse 3

Bildquellennachweis:

|Alamy Stock Photo (RMB), Abingdon/Oxfordshire: Ball, David 38.4; Hornak, Angelo 38.3; Kuttig 38.2; moyano, juan 3.17; Segre, Alex 35.6; Turner, Bob 38.6. |Colourbox.com, Odense: Monkey Business Images 35.2. |fotolia.com, New York: 300dpi 3.8; Kramin, V. 3.16; Licht und Blindheit 38.5; NilsZ 3.13; OHRAUGE 38.7; samuelkruszewski 36.8; sveta 3.12; zhu difeng 29.2; zjk 29.1. |iStockphoto.com, Calgary: Ferrao, José Manuel 3.15; gmnicholas 3.5; Grassetto 3.3; JohanJK 19.5; ma-k 3.7; simonbradfield 35.3; studiocasper 3.4. |Shutterstock.com, New York: Amat, Aaron 3.9; Barton, Willy 35.5; ESLINE 19.1; Heim, Ramona 19.8; Stockforlife 3.6; stockphoto-graf 3.14. |stock.adobe.com, Dublin: Ben-Ari, Rafael 35.4; emuck 3.11; Fischer, Magda 3.2; Kostic, Dusan 19.3; sergojpg 3.10. |Tauber, Andreas, Berlin: 5.3, 5.4, 5.5, 5.6, 5.7, 5.8, 5.9, 5.10, 5.11, 5.12, 5.13, 6.9, 6.10, 7.6, 7.19, 9.18, 9.19, 11.8, 15.17, 15.18, 18.1, 18.2, 18.3, 21.10, 21.11, 23.1, 26.2, 27.14, 27.15, 30.1, 30.2, 36.7, 37.2, 39.13, 39.14, 40.1, 40.2, 45.1. |vario images, Bonn: Uppercut 19.6.

Wir arbeiten sehr sorgfältig daran, für alle verwendeten Abbildungen die Rechteinhaberinnen und Rechteinhaber zu ermitteln. Sollte uns dies im Einzelfall nicht vollständig gelungen sein, werden berechtigte Ansprüche selbstverständlich im Rahmen der üblichen Vereinbarungen abgegolten.

Texte soweit nicht anders angegeben: Gisela Ehlers, Grit Kahstein, Christina Meindl, Ursula Michailow-Drews, Anna Van Montagu, Matthias Muth, Michaela Schönau, Hannelore Tait, Anne Zeich-Pelsis

Musiknachweis Pupil's Audio-CD:
1/2: Bumblebee rap ℗ © Westermann Bildungsmedien Verlag. **3/4:** The colour song ℗ © Westermann Bildungsmedien Verlag. **9/10:** Together. Text/Musik: Mark und Helen Johnson © Out of the Ark Ltd. Arrangement: Karl-F. Parnow-Kloth, ton-pumpe, Lüneburg ℗ Westermann Bildungsmedien Verlag. **14/15:** Harry the hamster. Text: Wolle Kriwanek / Musik und Arrangement: Wolle Kriwanek, Jörg Orlamünder, Michael Schwarz ℗ © Westermann Bildungsmedien Verlag. **17/18:** Reach for the sky. Text/Musik: Pamela Conn Beall, Susan Hagen Nipp © Price Sloan, an imprint of Penguin Publishing Group, a division of Penguin House LLC ℗ Westermann Bildungsmedien Verlag. **21/22:** Weekend is here. Text: Wolle Kriwanek / Musik und Arrangement: Wolle Kriwanek, Jörg Orlamünder, Michael Schwarz ℗ © Westermann Bildungsmedien Verlag. **25/26:** Animal rap ℗ © Westermann Bildungsmedien Verlag. **29/30:** Breakfast chant ℗ © Westermann Bildungsmedien Verlag. **38/39:** I hear them. Text/Musik: traditionell. ℗ © Westermann Bildungsmedien Verlag.

westermann GRUPPE

© 2021 Westermann Bildungsmedien Verlag GmbH, Braunschweig, www.westermann.de

Druck A[1] / Jahr 2021
Alle Drucke der Serie A sind im Unterricht parallel verwendbar.

Redaktion: Tisa Purackal, Lena Schmidt
Umschlaggestaltung: Visuelle Lebensfreude, Hannover, mit Illustrationen von Friederike Schumann
Layout: Visuelle Lebensfreude, Hannover
Druck und Bindung: Westermann Druck GmbH, Braunschweig

ISBN 978-3-14-**126901**-7